Modern World Religions

Buddhism

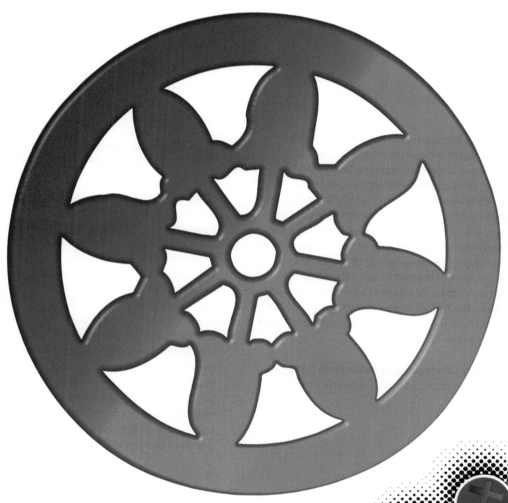

Anne Geldart

Heinemann

Heinemann Educational Publishers
Halley Court, Jordan Hill, Oxford, OX2 8EJ
a division of Reed Educational and Professional
Publishing Ltd

OXFORD MELBOURNE AUCKLAND
JOHANNESBURG BLANTYRE GABORONE
IBADAN PORTSMOUTH (NH) USA CHICAGO

Heinemann is a registered trademark of Reed
Educational and Professional Publishing Ltd

Text © Anne Geldart, 2002

First published in 2002

06 05 04 03 02
10 9 8 7 6 5 4 3 2 1

British Library Cataloguing in Publication Data
A catalogue record for this book is available from the
British Library

ISBN 0 435 33602 9

Picture research by Jennifer Johnson
Typeset by Artistix, Thame, Oxon
Printed and bound in Spain by Edelvive

Acknowledgements
The publishers would like to thank the following for
permission to use photographs: AKG London/Gilles
Mermet, p. 7; Andes Press Agency/C & D Hill, pp. 6 and
37 (bottom); Andes Press Agency/Carlos Reyes Manzo,
pp. 16, 18, 19, 27 (top), 30, 47 and 57; Robin Bath, pp. 3,
8, 23 (top), 24, 25, 27 (bottom), 31 (middle and right), 38
and 58; Camerapress/Benoit Gysembergh, p. 59;
Christine Osborne Pictures, pp. 10, 29, 34, 37 (top), 46, 48
(bottom), 50 and 52; Christine Osborne Pictures/Nick
Dawson, p. 39; Christine Osborne/P Kapoor, p. 23 (bottom);
Christine Osborne Pictures/S A Molton, p. 31 (left); Circa
Photo Library/William Holtby, pp. 26, 36 and 40;
Hutchison Library/Jon Burbank, p. 4 (bottom); Hutchison
Library/Jeremy Horner, p. 48 (top); Karuna Trust, p. 53;
Ann & Bury Peerless, p. 4 (top); Angela Walker, p. 41.

The publishers have made every effort to contact
copyright holders. However, if any material has been
incorrectly acknowledged, the publishers would be
pleased to correct this at the earliest opportunity.

Tel: 01865 888058 www.heinemann.co.uk

Websites
Links to appropriate websites are given throughout the
book. Although these were up-to-date at the time of
writing, it is essential for teachers to preview these sites
before using them with pupils. This will ensure that the
web address (URL) is still accurate and the content is
suitable for your needs. We suggest that you bookmark
useful sites and consider enabling pupils to access them
through the school intranet. We are bringing this to your
attention as we are aware of legitimate sites being
appropriated illegally by people wanting to distribute
unsuitable and offensive material. We strongly advise
you to purchase suitable screening software so that
pupils are protected from unsuitable sites and their
material. If you do find that the links given no longer
work, or the content is unsuitable, please let us know.
Details of changes will be posted on our website.

Contents

Introduction

In this section you will:
- learn about the Buddhist religion and its place in the world
- think about how religions influence society

A religion without a god?

Do you have to believe in a god to have a religion? Buddhists would say 'no'. **Buddhism** is a religion, but there is not a Buddhist god. Most Buddhists are **agnostic** – they do not think it is possible to know whether a god exists.

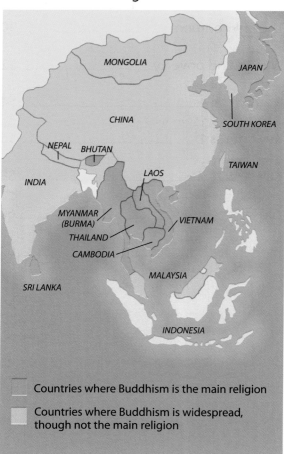

Countries where Buddhism is the main religion

Countries where Buddhism is widespread, though not the main religion

However, Buddhism is like many other religions. It has ideas about life and death, holy books, religious leaders, prayer, meditation and special ceremonies for birth, marriage and death.

How Buddhism began

In 563 BCE **Siddhartha Gautama** was born in India. About 35 years later, he travelled around India and became known as the **Buddha**. He died in 483 BCE.

His teachings spread to other countries such as Sri Lanka, Tibet and Nepal. Japan, China and Korea also converted to Buddhism. As you can see from the map on this page, Buddhism is a world-wide religion. Travellers who visited the East learned about Buddhism and returned to Britain to tell about this religion.

Early in the twentieth century, the Buddhist Society began in London. A well-known judge, Christmas Humphreys, was a member.

Buddhist ideas became popular among young people in the West in the 1960s. Buddhists are pacifist (anti-war) and vegetarian. They believe that humans should work out their own truths and not rely on a god. They believe in the re-birth of human beings and other life forms until they reach true happiness, or **nirvana**.

Musicians such as the Beatles used verses from the Buddhist books in their songs. Artists painted pictures using ideas from the **mandalas** and other Buddhist pictures.

Countries where Buddhism is the main religion today

An example of Buddhist art

Many other young people found out about Buddhism when they served in the armed forces in Vietnam. The film director, Oliver Stone, became a Buddhist when he was in Vietnam.

Other people in the West who are interested in Buddhism are the rock singer Tina Turner, the musician Suzanne Vega and film stars Richard Gere and Keanu Reeves. Films such as *Kundun* and *Little Buddha* have been very popular and show how interest in Buddhism goes on.

The **Dalai Lama** is the spiritual leader of all Buddhists and lived in Tibet. In the 1950s the Chinese invaded Tibet and he was forced into exile.

In Burma, Aung San Suu Kyi is a political leader and a Buddhist. She is well-known for standing up against a military government that took power when her own party had won the election.

Learning about religion

❶ Write down some of the ideas you have read about in this section that you think make Buddhism attractive. Give reasons for your answer.

❷ 'If it doesn't have a god, it can't be a religion.' How might a Buddhist answer this? What do you think? Give reasons for your answers.

Learning from religion

❶ Many Buddhists are vegetarian. Make two lists labelled 'good points' and 'bad points' about vegetarianism. Then read out your ideas in a class discussion.

❷ 'Buddhism is 2500 years old. It's ideas are out-of-date today.' Why do people disagree with this?

❸ Use the Internet, or a CD-ROM, to find out about a Buddhist country. Prepare a talk about that country, showing how important Buddhism is to its people.

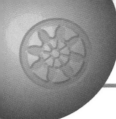

The birth of the Buddha

In this section you will:
- learn about the stories told about the Buddha's birth and their symbolic meanings
- think about the importance of birth and how it can give meaning.

Queen Mayadevi's dream

Queen Mayadevi's Dream

Some Buddhists believe that the **Buddha** lived through many other lifetimes, both human and animal, before he was born.

In the countries of India and Nepal there was a tribe called the **Saykas**. Their King **Suddhodana** was married to Queen **Mayadevi**. The Queen was not only beautiful, she was brave and good. One evening she felt great joy and peace. She told her husband about this, and asked him not to have sex with her for a while.

That night, as she slept, she had a dream about an elephant with six tusks and a red head.

Explaining the dream

In the morning she told the King about her dream. He called eight holy men to explain it. They told him that it was a good sign. It was a sign that the Buddha was coming into the world through the Queen's womb. He would be either a great emperor or a great holy man.

Lumbini Grove today

The birth of the Buddha

When the baby was due to be born, the King and Queen went for a walk in the wood of **Lumbini**. The Queen stepped from her carriage, followed by dancers and musicians. She came to a sala tree that bent down so that she could hold a branch.

The baby Buddha was born from her right side. Without any help, he walked seven steps to the North, then to the South, then to the East and then to the West. At each step a **lotus flower** sprang from the ground. His limbs shone like gold. He seemed to be surrounded with light.

He said, 'No further births will I have to suffer, for this is my last body. Now shall I destroy and pluck out the roots of sorrow that are caused by the wheel of birth, life and death.'

The King decided to call the child **Siddhartha**, which means 'Perfect Fulfilment' because on the day of his birth everything has become perfect.

When the baby was seven days old, his mother died. The King later married Mayadevi's sister, Mahapajapa. She looked after Siddhartha as if he were her own child.

A wise man called **Asita** came to visit the baby. He found 32 marks or signs on his body which showed that he would lead people to great truths. Asita wept because he knew that he would not live long enough to see the child become the man who would be such an important teacher.

The King was afraid of all this talk from priests and holy men. He decided to bring the boy up in the palace. This would prevent him leaving to take up the wandering life of a **monk**.

Learning about religion

❶ Make two lists: in one write the things that happen in the birth story of the Buddha. In the other write those that happen in the birth stories of Jesus. What is similar and what is different? (You can find help in Matthew 1 and 2, and Luke 1 and 2 in the New Testament.)

❷ Many Buddhists doubt whether the birth of the Buddha happened as the story says, but they still think it is important. What might the story tell you about the beliefs people have about the Buddha?

❸ Produce a newspaper called 'Palace News' with a story about the birth of the Buddha by the 'Palace reporter'.

Learning from religion

❶ Many religions have stories about dreams. Write about an important dream that you have had. Why was it important to you?

❷ What things would you think about when trying to choose a name for your child?

❸ 'The stories about the birth of the Buddha are unbelievable and can teach us nothing.' What might a Buddhist say about this? What do you think?

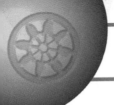

The discontented prince

In this section you will:
- learn how Prince Siddhartha became discontented with life in the palace
- understand why he thought it was important to search for meaning and truth.

Chained to unhappiness

Prince **Siddhartha** had everything he could want. His father gave him his own palace and servants.

One day he tried to save a swan from an arrow fired by one of his friends. The story shows how he cared for the bird. It also is a way of saying that he knew about unhappiness.

The King tried to stop him from ever knowing about pain. He even made sure that Siddhartha would not see servants who were ill or old.

The King thought that if Siddhartha saw these people he would ask questions that might lead him to a religious life. He was even banned from going into the city in case he saw the way things really were.

Siddhartha fell in love with a beautiful princess called **Yashodhara**. But when their first child was born, he named him **Rahula**, which means 'Chain'. This was a sign that he was unhappy.

Visits to the city

One day, Siddhartha persuaded **Channa**, the King's chariot-driver, to take him to the city.

On his first visit he saw an old man leaning on a stick. He asked what was wrong with him. Channa said 'He is old. One day we shall all be like him, both princes and ordinary people.'

On the second visit, Siddhartha saw a man who was ill, lying at the side of the road. Channa told him that everyone gets ill; it was a fact of life. On a third visit, he saw a dead man, lying and decaying at the side of the road. Channa explained that everyone dies.

Siddhartha was confused. Why had his father hidden such truths from him?

On a fourth visit to the city, he saw a bald man, carrying a bowl and wearing only a simple robe. Channa told him that this was a holy man, who had given up everything for the cause of truth.

Siddhartha decided that he must leave the palace in order to learn the truth. Early one morning, when everyone in the palace was deeply asleep, Siddhartha awoke. He wakened Channa, and ordered him to take him to where the holy man lived.

The young Prince Siddhartha

Siddhartha cuts off his hair before his enlightenment

As he got down from the chariot at the edge of the wood, Siddhartha gave his expensive cloak to Channa. He took a knife and cut off his long hair that he wore in a ponytail. Now he would begin his search for truth with the holy men.

Learning about religion

❶ Was Siddhartha's father really being loving when he tried to protect him from the outside world? Give reasons for your answer, showing that you have thought about more than one point of view.

❷ Some Buddhists think that Siddhartha saw visions of the old, the ill, the dead and the holy man – that he did not see them in the flesh. Does it make any difference? Give reasons for your answer.

Learning from religion

❶ How could someone like Siddhartha, who had everything he needed, be unhappy?

❷ Siddhartha left home to try to answer the big questions. What are the most important questions to you? Can they all be answered?

❸ 'It was not fair that Siddhartha left his family behind. It was selfish.' How might a Buddhist reply to this? What do you think?

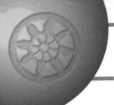

The enlightenment of the Buddha

In this section you will:

● learn about the enlightenment of the Buddha

● understand why this is important to Buddhists

A flash of inspiration

There is a story about the scientist Isaac Newton. He discovered the existence of gravity when an apple fell off a tree and hit him on the head.

Alexander Fleming noticed that some mould killed bacteria. As a result of his work we have penicillin. Scientists may suddenly see the truth about an event that no one else has noticed.

Religious people may have similar sudden flashes of inspiration. They may describe this as 'seeing the light' or '**enlightenment**'. They say you may have to wait years to have such a vision.

The enlightened Buddha

Siddhartha leaves the holy men

Ascetics are people who believe that if you live a strict life, with no bodily comfort, you can get to know the truth about life. **Siddhartha** joined a group of holy men who practised asceticism. He slept on thorns, ate mud and tried to live on no more than one grain of rice a day.

One day when he was meditating, he heard a passing music teacher talking to his pupil. He was saying 'If the strings are too tight, they will break and not play. If they are too slack, they will not play either.'

Siddhartha saw that he would not find the truth either in the life of luxury he had at the palace, or by denying himself as he was, living with the holy men. The truth must lie between the two extremes, he later called this the **Middle Way**.

Siddhartha went to the river and a local girl gave him a drink and some food. The holy men were disgusted and said he was a traitor.

The Middle Way lies between pain and pleasure

Siddhartha becomes the Buddha

Siddhartha left the men and went to a place called **Bodh Gaya**. He sat under a bodhi tree, waiting to reach full understanding of the big questions in life. There he had many visions. Buddhists believe that a devil called **Mara** tried to keep him from the truth.

First Mara sent his three daughters to distract Siddhartha. The three daughters were images of lust, ignorance and greed. Siddhartha ignored them. Then Mara made him believe that he was in the middle of a great storm, and then that he was under attack from an army. Siddhartha continued to meditate.

Finally, Mara appeared as an image of Siddhartha. Siddhartha was not fooled, and Mara gave up.

During that night, Siddhartha learned about other lives he had experienced. He came to understand about the nature of suffering, and that it was possible to be free from suffering. He found the truth of suffering in what he called the **Four Noble Truths**. He saw the **Eightfold Path** as a way to give people freedom or liberation.

He was no longer Siddhartha, but the **Buddha**. 'Buddha' means the 'enlightened one'.

Learning about religion

❶ Why do you think Mara tried to stop Siddhartha becoming the Buddha?

❷ 'The Buddha's experiences are helpful to people who seek enlightenment today.' Why might this be so?

Learning from religion

❶ How might the Middle Way be relevant today, even to those who are not Buddhists?

❷ Why do you think so many religions have some kind of devil figure?

❸ Are ideas like the Devil a way of not owning up to our own bad choices? What do you think? Give reasons.

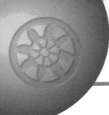

The death of the Buddha

The Buddha as a teacher

For 45 years the **Buddha** travelled in India teaching his ideas. People followed him and became his disciples. These included the holy men who had called him a traitor, as well as his son, **Rahula**, and another man, **Ananda**.

The story of Kisagami

'We die all the time, from moment to moment, and what is really there is a perpetual succession of extremely short-lived events.'

Edward Conze

What this quotation means is that over seven years every cell in the body dies and is replaced by another. This is a way in which we are dying all the time. We need to learn how to deal with this fact.

Kisagami was an unhappy woman. Her child had died, and she still carried him around. She came to the Buddha and

ဘုရားသည် ဗာရာဏသီ ပြည် အနီးရှိ မိဂဒါဝန် တောၡ္ ကောဋ္ဌည-ဝပ္ပ-ဘဒ္ဒိယ-မဟာနာမ-အဿဇိ ဟူသော ပဉ္စဝဂ္ဂီ ၎ါ:ဦ:တို့
ရှင်ကောဋ္ဌညသည် ဦ:စွာသောတုန်:အဖြစ်သို့ရောက်ပြီ: အနတ္တလက္ခဏသုတ်ကို ဆက်လက်ရှိဟောတော်ရ ပဉ္စဝဂ္ဂ
ဖြစ်လာကြသဖြင့် ဘုရား:ရှင်၏ သာသနာတွင်ပထမဦ:ဆုံ:သောသံယာတော်များ ဖြစ်ကြလေသည်။

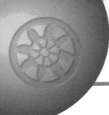

ဘ်.ဦ:ဉတ္တယသာရ-မြိနယ် သံယာနာယက္ကအဖွဲ့အမှုဆောင်-ကောဓမယ်ကိကိဓကာင်:ကော

The Buddha and his disciples

asked him to perform a miracle and cure her son.

The Buddha saw that she had not accepted that her child was dead. He gave her a task to help her to face this fact.

'Go and collect mustard seeds from every house where death has not visited, and then return with them and I will help you,' he said.

Kisagami went knocking on many doors. But the answer was always the same. Over the years, many people had died in every house that she visited.

Kisagami returned to the Buddha and placed the body of her child at his feet. She had tears in her eyes, because she now accepted that she was not alone in her loss, and that everyone has to experience death.

The Buddha told her to bury the child. Kisagami became a Buddhist from that day on.

The death of the Buddha

When the Buddha was 80 years old he died. He had been telling his assistant, Ananda, that he would soon die, but Ananda could not accept it. The Buddha visited a follower called **Chunda**. While there, the Buddha ate something, probably a mushroom, which gave him food poisoning.

He invited his disciples to come and stay at **Kusingara**, where Buddhists believe he entered **nirvana** at the time of his death.

The Buddha was to be **cremated**, that is, his body would be burned to ashes. The funeral **pyre** was not lit until the Malian **monks** were able to reach the place.

When the Buddha died, there was music, dancing and rejoicing. He had led many people to the truth. It seemed wrong to be sad.

In his teaching he said that people are born, decay and die, but they continue and are re-born in another place.

After the fire died down, traditional stories say that there were 84,000 **relics** of the Buddha. These are preserved in Buddhist temples in many places in Asia.

Learning about religion

❶ Write an obituary (appreciation of his life) for the Buddha as if you were writing for a Buddhist newspaper.

❷ Write a poem about the story of Kisagami.

Learning from religion

❶ 'True **Buddhism** died with the death of the Buddha.' Do you agree? Give reasons for your answer.

❷ Is thinking about death an unhealthy thing to do? Give reasons for your answer.

❸ What would you like people to remember about you after you have gone? Try writing a short obituary for yourself.

Buddhist teaching on suffering

In this section you will:

● learn about the Four Noble Truths and the Eightfold Path

● think about how to deal with suffering.

The Buddha's teaching

The **Buddha** taught that there were **Four Noble Truths**. These are:

1. Everyone suffers. Birth, illness, old age and death are all painful, and come to all people.

2. The cause of pain and suffering is desire.

3. Pain will cease if people learn not to desire. This is called non-attachment.

4. Non-attachment can come about if people learn to follow the **Eightfold Path**.

The Buddha thought that when human beings want to own things, have relationships with other people, or long for things, this will cause pain. This is because what they long for is not permanent; it does not last.

Most of these longings are selfish. He said that people must learn that there is no such thing as self. Human beings are a number of parts and events that come together for a time. It is a continuous process.

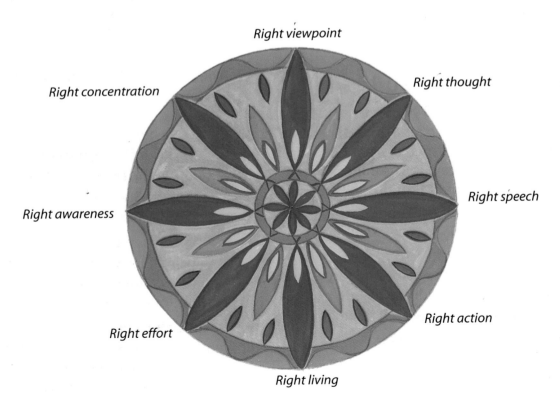

Right viewpoint

Right thought

Right concentration

Right speech

Right awareness

Right action

Right effort

Right living

The Eightfold Path

Another Buddhist, **Nagasena**, compared the self with a chariot. He said that a chariot is not a thing on its own. It is a collection of parts, such as wheels and an axle.

What human beings know as 'self' is a mixture of love, anger, humour, wisdom and other qualities. These become separated when humans die, in the same way that dandelion seeds are scattered by the wind.

The Buddha said that people believe an illusion and hope that they are always going to remain the same. Buddhists believe that they can end suffering if they see beyond this false image of what life is about, and follow the Eightfold Path.

The Eightfold Path is not eight separate steps, but eight parts of a way of living. These are:

1. **Right Understanding**: Buddhists must understand the truths that the Buddha has taught.

2. **Right Intention**: Buddhists must make sure that they always act for the right reasons.

3. **Right Speech**: Buddhists must speak in a way that is harmless and is not rude or dishonest. They must not keep talking about themselves.

4. **Right Action**: They must live according to the **Five Moral Precepts** (see page 14) as taught by the Buddha.

5. **Right Occupation**: They must choose a job that does not encourage them to be arrogant or violent. Most Buddhists would not want to be a butcher or a soldier for this reason.

Learning about religion

1. Draw a diagram to show how the 'self' is made up of different parts.

2. Write a paragraph about which of the Four Noble Truths or the Eightfold Path are most difficult to believe or to follow.

3. 'The Eightfold Path is really a set of rules in disguise.' What would a Buddhist think about this?

Learning from religion

1. 'Desire leads to pain.' Write about the different ways that we use the word 'pain'.

2. 'It would be impossible for anyone fully to live out the idea of Right Speech.' Do you think people should try to carry out this idea? Give reasons for your answer.

6. **Right Effort**: This is not about 'making an effort', but by using **meditation** to make sure they do the right things and do not dwell on the outcomes of their effort.

7. **Right Mindfulness**: this is a kind of mind control. Through meditation a Buddhist can become especially aware of all that they do in thought, speech and action.

8. **Right Concentration**: By using the right form of meditation, Buddhists can be free from worry, anxiety and envy. This will enable them to think clearly and reach **nirvana**.

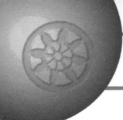

Five Moral Precepts

In this section you will:

● learn about the Five Moral Precepts

● think about whether it is better to have good intentions, or to keep promises.

Avoid taking what is not given

Good intentions

Generally, people think it is important to keep promises. People who cannot keep promises about small things may not be able to keep their word on big things. The **Buddha** asked his followers to have five intentions. He gave them five targets to aim for in living a good life. They are called the **Five Moral Precepts**.

Five intentions

The Buddha made suggestions for his followers, rather than laying down rules. These were:

1 **To avoid taking life**. This applies to both animals and humans. Many Buddhists are therefore vegetarian and pacifists (anti-war). This also means that Buddhists must think carefully about abortion and euthanasia. Buddhists believe in the principle of **ahimsa** or harmlessness.

2 **To avoid taking what is not given**. Some Buddhists think that this does not just apply to stealing property. It is also about stealing someone else's ideas or their reputation. This might

happen when people claim the credit for something that someone else actually did.

3 **To avoid sexual misconduct**. The idea of ahimsa applies to the way people treat one another. They should try not to hurt one another. Many believe that sex should only happen within a committed relationship, such as marriage. This is because sex for the wrong reasons can cause pain to another person.

4 **To avoid speaking falsely**. Buddhists believe that people should always tell the truth, speak quietly, and respectfully. They think that it is important to listen to other people's point of view. They think it is wrong to lie, or to hurt people by saying nasty things to them or about them.

Avoid speaking falsely and gossiping

5 **To avoid drink and drugs that can cloud the mind**. Buddhists believe that it is 'unskilful', that is, unhelpful, to get drunk or to take drugs for the wrong reasons. They do not object to drugs for medical reasons. They believe that taking drugs to get high or to forget their problems is not helpful. It is a way of avoiding reality rather than facing up to it.

The Buddha believed that if people keep to these intentions, they would grow in wisdom and understanding. They would learn what is **skilful** (or right) and what is **lacking in skill** (or likely to cause suffering).

The Buddha taught that if people follow the Five Moral Precepts, they would develop **karuna**. Karuna is a **compassionate** love for all living creatures.

Learning about religion

❶ What do ahimsa and karuna mean? How easy is it to follow these principles?

❷ Arrange the Five Moral Precepts in the order in which you consider to be most important.

Learning from religion

❶ What do you understand by 'speaking falsely'? How might speaking falsely hurt other people?

❷ Do you think it is easier to have suggestions for right living, or a set of rules that people have to obey? Give reasons for your answer.

15

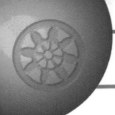

Nirvana, karma and re-birth

In this section you will:

● learn about nirvana, karma and re-birth

● ask what people mean by 'paradise'.

The promise of a paradise

Human beings often dream of a place where they can be happy. It would be a place where life is pleasant and easy and where everyone can live a good life. This dream place would be 'Paradise'.

Buddhists believe that their aim is to reach **nirvana**. This is a state of being, not a place. They believe that this is when they have finally left behind 'self', and have become one with the universe.

Re-birth

Buddhists believe that human beings are trapped in a **wheel of life**. They believe that people are re-born many times. Each time is a fresh opportunity to reach nirvana. When they reach nirvana, they can be free from suffering or the business of 'being'. Buddhists think that we cannot know, but individuals may be re-born in different forms. It may be as a person, an animal or even a plant. A re-birth could be in a particular form to teach a quality that is missing. For example, an angry or impatient person may be re-born as a tree to teach them to be still and wait.

Nirvana is the spiritual equivalent of paradise

If a person is re-born as a human being, this is an opportunity not to be wasted.

This is because only human beings have the mental ability to reach **enlightenment** (see page 8).

What goes around, comes around

We have all done something bad, or said something nasty and this has caused trouble. On the other hand, we may have done something kind for someone else. This makes us feel good when we see them benefit from our actions.

Buddhists believe that the kind of re-birth a person has depends on their **karma**. Karma can be good or bad. Good karma comes from doing good, and bad karma is from doing bad things. If people do good, then good will follow. If they do evil, then bad things will follow. 'As you sow, so shall you reap.' People can feel the results of karma in their present lifetime.

In **Buddhism**, karma can be carried forward into another lifetime. It is therefore very important to live the best life possible. People can end up carrying karma from many lifetimes. It is karma that decides whether people reach enlightenment, or whether they have to live a thousand lives as a lower life-form in order to reach the truth.

Karma can work for whole nations, as well as individuals. Buddhists call this collective karma. They would say that the way rich nations treat the poorer nations can affect the karma of a whole country.

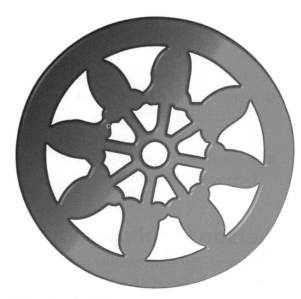

The wheel of life

Learning about religion

❶ What do Buddhists mean by 'nirvana' and 'karma'?

❷ How is this different from ideas of 'paradise' that other people might have?

❸ Draw a diagram to explain re-birth, based on the 'wheel of life'.

Learning from religion

❶ Do you think that all actions have consequences? Give an example from your own life.

❷ Write a story about someone who thinks they have been re-born.

The Three Refuges

In this section you will:
- learn about the Three Refuges, and how these are important to Buddhists
- think about how important it is to belong to a community.

A person to follow

We all rely on different people to help us. A police officer can warn us of traffic problems. A tour guide can tell us what to expect on our holiday. A team coach will give us advice and support for our sport.

Buddhists believe in the **Three Refuges** (sometimes called the three jewels). A refuge is a place of safety. Buddhists believe that these refuges exist within a person.

The **Buddha** is expressed in the sentence:

'I go to the Buddha for refuge.'

A Buddha is a person who is aware of the way the world is, who is wise and can see clearly. Buddhists believe that people can learn from experience. If they have taken a particular pathway to deal with a situation, they can reflect on this. This helps them to see clearly and find a better way to do things. They develop *insight*. Insight is a person's gut feeling, or inner voice. It is their wisdom. They have learned to trust their own judgement. They can find refuge in the confidence that these feelings bring.

The Dharma

The second refuge is:

'I go to the **Dharma** for refuge.'

The Dharma is the Buddhist name for the teachings of the Buddha. The word 'dharma' means 'universal truth'. This is a challenge to live according to this truth. The Dharma is written in Buddhist scriptures.

Buddhists may consult **monks**, who are specially trained in the scriptures, if they need guidance about the teachings of the Buddha. They may meditate to try to find the truth for themselves.

The symbol for the Three Refuges

Reading the Dharma

We all have a need to belong to a group

Some Buddhists, such as Zen Buddhists, have teachers who are especially wise and tell stories to help them to understand the Dharma.

The Sangha

Everyone needs to feel that they belong to a group. This makes them feel secure. Families and friends help you when you are in need, and stick by you when you are in trouble.

The third of the three refuges is:

'I go to the **Sangha** for refuge.'

Buddhists believe that it is important to belong to a Sangha. They can then take part in the festivals and celebrations of their religion. They can share their thoughts and insights gained through prayer and meditation. They can share problems. A Sangha is a community of friends with similar beliefs who try to support each other in the development of their faith.

Learning about religion

❶ Design a leaflet to explain the importance of the three refuges to Buddhists.

❷ 'You could be a good Buddhist without joining a group.' What do you think a Buddhist would say to this?

Learning from religion

❶ In what ways do people try to make themselves happy and secure? Do you think these things work? Explain your answer.

❷ What are the three most important things in your life? Explain your selection.

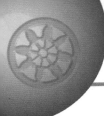

Types of Buddhism

In this section you will:
● learn about the similarities and differences between the two main kinds of Buddhism
● think about why differences develop within groups.

Witness to a crime

Imagine someone has committed a crime. When it comes to a trial, witnesses may disagree about many details. They may not agree about the facts, or the order in which events happened.

However, in a court of law, it is possible to convict someone, even if witnesses do not agree. The Magistrate or the Jury can form a picture of the truth.

The blind men and the elephant

Blind men and elephants

A famous Buddhist story tells of a King who asked a group of blind men to feel a part of an elephant and then describe it. The one who held the trunk thought it was like a snake. The one who touched the leg thought it was like a tree, and so on. They did not describe the elephant as it really was. Together they could give enough information to get at the truth.

Buddhists would say that the different groups within **Buddhism** cannot get to the whole truth by themselves. They can only point towards the truth.

A witness to a crime can be important

Theravada Buddhism

'**Theravada**' means 'the teaching of the elders'. It looks to the teachings of the **Buddha** in the **Pali Canon**, which is the first, original scripture of Buddhism. This group exists mainly in south east Asia.

Theravada Buddhists believe that the Buddha was a man and not superhuman.

They believe that people who want to follow a religious life as **monks** and **nuns** find it easier if the **Sangha** supports them. They aim to follow the six perfections to achieve **merit**. The six perfections are:

- morality (**sila**)
- generosity (**dana**)
- patience (**kshanti**)
- energy (**virya**)
- concentration (**dhyana**)
- wisdom (**prajna**).

Mahayana Buddhism

Mahayana Buddhism began in the first century BCE. It is found in Korea, Tibet and China. Mahayana Buddhists believe that everyone can become a Buddha. They believe that the Buddha was a special person.

They say that the Buddha had three bodies:

a Transformation body – the body he had when he was alive.

b Enjoyment body – the body people see when he visits them in visions today.

c Thought body – the body in which he will appear in a future time.

Mahayana Buddhists also teach about the **Bodhisattvas**. These are Buddhists who have achieved **enlightenment**, but who stay behind in this world to help lead others to the truth. They are already 'Buddhas to be'. They may be compared to spiritual beings.

There are other types of Buddhism too. Nichiren Shoshu is named after a thirteenth century monk called Nichiren Daishonin. Nichiren Daishonin believed that he completed the Buddha's message.

Learning about religion

❶ What do you think the Buddha would say about there being different types of Buddhism? Give your reasons.

❷ Use the Internet, or a CD-ROM, to help you find out more about one of the Buddhist countries. You could carry this out as group work and produce a report.

Learning from religion

❶ How can people who have different beliefs live alongside one another in peace?

❷ 'Religion says it wants to bring people together, but it always tears them apart.' Organize a class debate on this topic.

Buddhist symbols

The lotus flower

For Buddhists the **lotus flower** has the meaning 'transformation'. It is the symbol for purity and growth. The lotus flower floats on the surface of a lake and is very beautiful.

Its roots are buried deep in the mud at the bottom of the lake. The **Buddha** thought that this was like human life. People may be stuck in the mud of human existence, but we can still reach up towards **enlightenment**.

An important Buddhist scripture is called the **Lotus Sutra**. Some Buddhists sit in the lotus position (a yoga exercise) when they meditate. It helps them to gain peace.

The wheel of life

(see page 16)

The **wheel of life** is another important Buddhist symbol. It has eight spokes that stand for the **Eightfold Path**. It reminds Buddhists that they are trapped in the cycle of death and re-birth. They can only escape from this when they are no longer attached to 'being'. Once they achieve **nirvana**, they can be free from earth-bound being and be at one with the universe.

In the centre of the wheel are the cockerel, the snake and pig. These stand for greed, hatred and ignorance, or delusion.

Meditating in the lotus position helps Buddhists to gain peace

Over the top of the wheel is Yama, a demon. This reminds Buddhists that the world is subject to change and decay. The six 'realms' inside the wheel show the stages to enlightenment. In each one there is a Buddha. This means that a person can find enlightenment at any stage and in any place, if they truly wish to find it.

Buddha rupas

There are many different images of the Buddha. These are called **rupas**.

A sitting Buddha shows the importance of **meditation**. Buddha in the lotus position shows him teaching the **Dharma**.

Other images remind Buddhists of their religious teachings. For example, a horse without a rider reminds them of when the Buddha left the palace to join the holy men.

Making a mandala

Another way of showing beauty in a world of constant change is by making **mandalas**. Mandalas are pictures and patterns made from coloured sand, which remind Buddhists that nothing lasts forever.

A sitting Buddha rupa

Learning about religion

❶ Write a story about a person to show the idea of the lotus as a symbol for transformation, purity and growth.

❷ Design your own wheel of life which shows the Buddhist teaching.

Learning from religion

❶ Draw and colour a symbol for 'wisdom'.

❷ 'Making mandalas is really pointless.' What do you think?

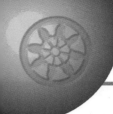

The Bodhisattvas

In this section you will:
- learn about the Bodhisattvas and their importance to Mahayana
- think about the importance of role models in your own personal development.

Avalokitesvara

Heroes or zeros

Many people enjoy stories about heroes and superheroes such as Superman. We may admire their strength and courage.

We may admire a famous sports player or a pop star. We may collect newspaper cuttings and magazines about them. We might try to live our lives as they do. They can be role models of how to live a good life. But they may be people who live a bad life, and lead us astray. We need to be careful in our choice of role model.

Enlightened beings

In **Mahayana Buddhism** there are beings called **Bodhisattvas** (see page 21). These are '**Buddhas** to be'. That is, they are beings who have gained **enlightenment**, but who hold back from **nirvana** so that they can lead others to enlightenment. Sometimes these beings may return as human beings. Tibetan Buddhists think that the **Dalai Lama** is a Bodhisattva.

Bodhisattvas may be seen as symbols for a quality that the Buddha had. They show what the individual Buddha should try to obtain. The most important of these qualities are wisdom and compassion.

Avalokitesvara

This Bodhisattva stands for perfect compassion or kindness. He wants to help Buddhists to find answers to their problems in daily living, as well as leading them to the goals of enlightenment and nirvana.

Tara

Buddhists believe that the Bodhisattva **Tara** sprouted from the side of **Avalokitesvara**. She helps in the process of enlightenment.

Tara

Maitreya

Many Buddhists think that **Maitreya** is the most important Bodhisattva, as he will one day come to earth and bring a 'golden age' of peace and wisdom. His teachings will be so wise and his leadership so powerful that he will be known as the second Buddha. He lives now in a heavenly state. People who have great religious experiences may meet him and he will reveal truths and lead them to enlightenment.

Learning about religion

❶ Why are Bodhisattvas so important to many Buddhists? What problems might a Buddhist have who relies on Bodhisattvas?

❷ 'Bodhisattvas are really gods by another name.' What might a Buddhist say to this? What do you think? Give reasons for your answer.

Learning from religion

❶ Write about a person you regard as a role model. Say why they are important to you.

❷ Organize a class debate on the statement 'Compassion is more important than wisdom.'

You will need two people to speak *for* the motion, and two *against*. Finally the class can vote on which side they think has given the best case.

Maitreya

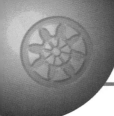

Buddhist devotion

In this section you will:
- discover some important aspects of Buddhist devotion, or 'paying respect'
- think about things that matter to you most.

What's it worth?

Many people are 'fans'. They take something or someone very seriously. It may be a football team, in which case they want to own the right shirt, have all the kit and a poster, of course! They want to watch as many games as possible, either live or on television.

Some may be followers of a music group or a singer. They want posters, CDs and, best of all, to see their pop idol live in concert.

Showing respect to the Buddha

Paying respect at home

Buddhists visit a **vihara** (temple) or **monastery** to help them in their religion. Many Buddhists also have a shrine in their home. This is a personal place for devotion. It has an image of the **Buddha** (called a **rupa**), flowers, candles, incense and pictures of **Bodhisattvas**.

Buddhist family members will recite the three jewels and the **Five Moral Precepts** at the shrine. They may meditate in front of it to help them to concentrate. They may burn incense to show their devotion to the Buddha.

Prayer

Many Buddhists do not think of their devotion as prayer. The Buddha is not a god, and **Buddhism** does not teach about a god.

When Buddhists pay respect, they feel that it 'releases the Buddha within'. This means that it releases the true nature of what is inside a person. Some think of this as a form of **meditation**, others say that it is showing respect to the Buddha.

A Buddhist named Dr Fernado once said:

'Prayer doesn't exist in Buddhism because there is no one to talk to. In my devotions, I say to myself "To the best of my ability, I shall try to emulate [copy] the life of the Buddha"'.

Flags and wheels

One kind of devotion is the reciting of a **mantra**, which is a short statement of faith.

Tibetan prayer wheels

In some Buddhist countries, you may see flags with a word or thought from a mantra written on them. When the wind blows, Buddhists believe that the energy contained in the thought is carried in the wind.

Some Buddhists use prayer wheels to release the prayers into the surrounding area.

Beads and bells

Many Buddhists use **mala beads** to help them to meditate. There are 108 of these on a string. They feel these help them to concentrate and to get rid of thoughts that intrude on their devotions.

You often hear bells in Buddhist countries. In Tibet, a bell is a symbol of wisdom.

Learning about religion

❶ Draw some of the important objects used in devotion mentioned in this unit. Explain how they are used.

❷ Which items used in Buddhist devotions do you find most interesting? Explain your choice.

Learning from religion

❶ What is the thing in your life you are most devoted to? Explain why.

❷ 'Prayer is a waste of time.' Write a speech or an article for your school magazine about this. Show you have thought about it from more than one point of view.

Meditation

Think it through

If you get stuck with a Maths problem, you may have to think about it very hard before you find a solution.

We often need to think things through before taking action that may bring harmful or negative consequences.

Buddhist meditation

It was through **meditation** that the **Buddha** achieved **enlightenment** (see page 8). Buddhists today use meditation to help them to understand problems. Meditation is a kind of training for the mind. The following are examples of how a Buddhist might meditate.

Breathe in slowly through your nose. As you do this, feel relaxed. Fix your mind

Thinking it through

A monk meditating: meditation is an important Buddhist practice

on breathing, so that you do not think about anything else. Breathe out – and feel the tensions leave your body. Try to concentrate on the rhythm of your breathing.

Imagine you are in a large room. Try to see all your family and friends around you.

Now picture someone you do not like. Instead of feeling hatred or anger, think warm thoughts about them.

Meditation can help Buddhists to understand the meaning of the teachings of the Buddha. It can help them to become aware of parts of their lives that need to be changed or developed. It helps them to develop clear thinking, understanding and

calm. Meditation can lead to freedom from suffering.

When Buddhists meditate, they may concentrate on some ideas that the Buddha thought were helpful. These ideas are called the **Brahma Viharas**, or 'spiritual friends'. They are personal qualities that are good to develop. They include:

1. **Metta**, or loving kindness – to be gentle and kind to all.

2. **Karuna,** or compassion – to have understanding and concern for others.

3. **Mudita,** or sympathetic joy – showing delight in the success of others.

4. **Upekka,** or composure – showing a balanced approach to life.

People can meditate alone or in groups. Buddhists may do this at the local Buddhist centre or temple.

Learning about religion

1. 'Meditation is a waste of time.' How would a Buddhist reply to this?

2. 'The Brahma Viharas are a good idea, but impossible to develop.' How might a Buddhist respond to this?

Learning from religion

1. Write down the feelings you had when you carried out the two meditations. Why do you think you reacted in these ways?

2. Give examples of how a person could show the Brahma Viharas in everyday life.

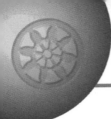

Buddhist holy places

The vihara

Most religious people have important places where they go to meet together to share their religion. One Buddhist place of meeting is the **vihara**.

The vihara may be part of a **monastery**. It has a shrine room where Buddhists meet. They meditate there and celebrate important festivals.

There are several important items in a shrine room. There is almost always a statue of the **Buddha**. Buddhists focus on this because it helps them with **meditation**.

Buddhists often place flowers, and light incense sticks and candles near the statue.

The smoke from the incense sticks represents truth (**Dharma**). Buddhists light these to show that they mean to live a life of good deeds and truthfulness. The candle is a symbol of wisdom and self-knowledge that the Buddha encouraged in his followers.

A Buddhist vihara

A wat in Wimbledon

A stupa in Thailand

A pagoda in Battersea

Other types of building

Buddhists have special buildings for meetings to pay respect to the Buddha. Some people call these places temples. In Thailand they are called a **wat**.

The picture shows a **stupa**, shaped like a bell. Stupas contain **relics** from the Buddha or an important Buddhist leader.

The temple in Kandy in Sri Lanka contains a tooth of the Buddha. It is a place of **pilgrimage**.

A **pagoda** is another important Buddhist building. It has five sections to remind Buddhists that the universe has five elements: earth, fire, water, wind and space.

Shrines at home

Buddhists meditate and show **devotion** to the Buddha at home as well as at viharas or temples. They may set aside a space, or even an entire room in their home, as places in which to meditate and show devotion.

Learning about religion

❶ Draw and label a diagram of the shrine room in a Buddhist temple. Explain what each of the important symbols means.

❷ 'You don't need holy buildings to be a Buddhist.' How would a Buddhist reply to this? What do you think?

❸ Write a poem, or draw five small pictures, to show what Buddhists believe about the elements of the universe.

Learning from religion

❶ What places are important to you? Why is this?

❷ Buddhist holy places can be full of noise or very quiet. Which would you prefer, and why?

Buddhist scriptures

In this section you will:
- learn about some holy writings important to Buddhists
- consider the importance of learning from the past.

Preserving the past

There are many ways that we can learn about the past. **Archaeologists** may dig up items from long ago. Books and other writings are important tools for learning about the past, too.

The Three Baskets

The chants, or verses, sung by the **Sangha** preserve the **Buddha's** teachings. Early Buddhists did not think that it was important to write down the stories of the Buddha. This only came about 500 years after the Buddha died.

During the first 500 years, the stories were passed down by word of mouth. People in those days were able to remember a lot of material. This was partly because fewer people were able to read and write.

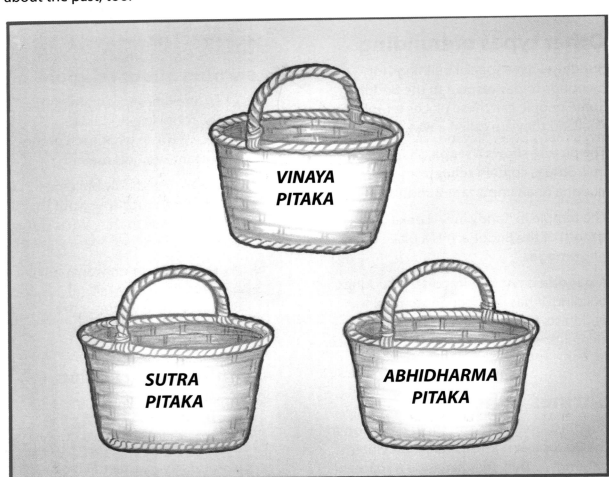

The Three Baskets

In 30 BCE a group of **monks** met on the island of Sri Lanka. They put together a book that is now called the **Tripitaka**, or Three Baskets.

The Three Baskets are:

1 The **Vinaya Pitaka** – these are the 227 rules that monks and **nuns** must follow, and how these rules were made.

2 The **Sutra Pitaka** – this is a collection of the words of the Buddha – his teachings.

3 The **Abhidharma Pitaka** – this is a collection of other teachings about how we look at the world around us.

Other scriptures

The Jataka Tales

This is a collection of 540 stories about the Buddha. Buddhists believe that the Buddha lived many other lifetimes before he died. He lived as different animals and humans. The **Jataka Tales** are about these other lives.

The Dharmapada

This is an important scripture which brings together some of the Buddha's sayings.

'One should give up anger – one should abandon pride.'

Verse 221

'Better than a thousand useless words is one word that brings peace.'

Verse 100

(sayings from the Dharmapada)

In the first century CE Buddhists in India began to collect teachings from the time of the Buddha. In China they began their collection of teachings a century later.

There are other important books in **Buddhism** which take the Buddha's teachings a stage further. One of these is the Tibetan *Book of the Dead*. This helps people to think about the consequences of their present life, and to prepare for their next life.

Learning about religion

1 Draw a diagram and label it, to show the Three Baskets and what they contain.

2 There were five hundred years between the death of the Buddha and the first collection of Buddhist holy books. Does this matter? Show you have thought about this from more than one point of view.

Learning from religion

1 'Buddhist holy books are so old, they have no meaning for people today.' What would a Buddhist say about this? What do you think?

2 Look at one of the sayings from the Dharmapada. Write a short play to show the meaning of the saying. (Your teacher might allow you to act this out with members of your study group.)

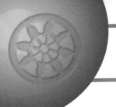

The festival of Wesak

In this section you will:

● learn about the Buddhist festival of Wesak

● discover how important it is to Buddhist people.

Celebrations

Everyone enjoys a festival! It is important to have time to have a party or to celebrate, to mark important events in the year. It may be New Year, a birthday, or an important sporting event. When we enjoy the good things in life, it is like saying that life if good and that it is worth living. Celebrations show what we think is important.

Wesak

Wesak (some Buddhists call it '**Buddha Day**') is the most important festival of the Buddhist year. Buddhists believe that the most important events in the life of the Buddha – his birth, his **enlightenment** and when he died – all happened on the

Washing images of the Buddha

same day in different years. So they celebrate the Buddha's special day at the time of the full moon, in May or June.

Wesak in Thailand

In Thailand Wesak is very important. There, Buddhists visit a **monastery**. They take flowers, a candle and an incense stick. The flowers are a sign that nothing lasts forever. The candle's melted wax has the same message. The candle's burning wick is a sign of wisdom. The incense is a sign of truth and **devotion** to the Buddha.

People walk around the **stupa** three times. This action shows their commitment to the Buddha, the **Dharma** and the **Sangha** in their lives. Some pour water round a bodhi tree (see page 9). This reminds them that the Buddha came to understand the truth while sitting under a tree like this.

To prepare for the festival of Wesak, Buddhists clean their houses thoroughly. They wash the statues of the Buddha. If they caught fish some days before, they let them go back into the river. This shows that the Buddha's teachings bring freedom. They set birds free from cages as another sign that they are celebrating freedom.

Wesak in Sri Lanka

In Sri Lanka, the people put huge paintings of events in the life of the Buddha on display. They hang lanterns in the street. There are acrobats and dancers performing in the street.

It is a great time for people to share the best things in life. There are wayside stalls of food and drink for people who have travelled a long way to come to the festival.

Learning about religion

❶ Why do you think that Wesak is so important to Buddhists?

❷ Choose three symbols or three actions performed at the festival of Wesak. Draw pictures with captions to explain them.

❸ 'The Buddha would have disapproved of Wesak.' What do you think?

Learning from religion

❶ 'People need celebrations.' Draw a spider diagram to show as many reasons as you can for celebrating.

❷ 'All these festivals prove that **Buddhism** is a religion like all others.' Look at the information on Wesak and the other festivals (see page 36–7) and say what you think. Give reasons for your answer.

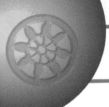

Other Buddhist festivals

In this section you will:
- learn about the meaning and traditions concerning other important Buddhist festivals
- think again about the need for festivals in our lives.

New Year

Many people, religious and non-religious, celebrate New Year. They use this time to think about the past year and to look forward to the future. Some people make an effort to change or improve themselves in the year ahead.

Songkran

For Buddhists in Thailand, New Year takes place in the middle of April. They celebrate this in the festival of **Songkran**. This festival uses water as part of the celebration. Thai people splash each other with water as a sign of a new start. There are colourful parades, boat races, masks and dances. Each village elects a princess of the festival.

When the festival ends, Thai people put on new clothes.

They also release fish into the rivers as a sign of the freedom that **enlightenment** brought to the **Buddha**.

Festival of the Tooth

Buddhists in Sri Lanka believe that a special **stupa** holds one of the Buddha's teeth. The tooth is inside a set of caskets.

This takes place on the night of the full moon in August. There are processions of

Songkran can get you very wet

·lephants at the Festival of the Tooth

·elephants. One of the elephants is dressed
·n golden materials. There are dancers,
·ugglers and other street entertainers.

*Obon is a time to remember those who have
died*

Obon

In Japan, Buddhists celebrate the festival of
Obon on 13 July. It reminds Buddhists of a
time when the Buddha rescued the mother
of one of his disciples from a kind of hell.

Japanese people have great respect for
their ancestors. During Obon they clean
the memorial stones of their dead
relatives with water, and put flowers on
the memorial stones.

The family members offer prayers for their
dead relatives, and burn incense to
encourage the spirits to return to the
world from which they came.

The festival ends when they light a huge
bonfire at Daimonjiyama, which is a
monastery on a holy mountain outside
the city of Kyoto.

Learning about religion

❶ Draw a series of small pictures to
show what happens during the
festival of Songkran.

❷ Do you think the Buddha would
be pleased with the Festival of
the Tooth? Explain your answer.

❸ Why do you think ancestors are so
important to Japanese Buddhists?

Learning from religion

❶ Why do you think people make
New Year resolutions?

❷ Many religions have a special
time to remember their dead
ancestors. Do you think this is a
good idea? Give reasons.

Buddhist pilgrimage

In this section you will:
- learn about some Buddhist places of pilgrimage
- think about the importance of special places to people.

We all need a place to get away to…

Special places

We all need to get away from the stress of normal life sometimes. We take holidays in places where we expect to find rest and relaxation.

Lumbini Grove

'The place, **Ananda**, at which the devoted person can say, "Here the **Buddha** was born" is a spot to be visited with feelings of reverence.'

The Buddha was born in **Lumbini Grove** in Nepal. Buddhists believe that when he was born the earth shook and was filled with light. He spent his young life in the area.

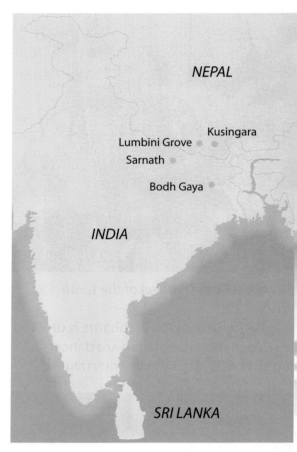

Places of Buddhist pilgrimage

The Buddhist King Asoka built a pillar to show that the Buddha was born there.

When **Siddhartha Gautama** was sitting under the bodhi tree at **Bodh Gaya** he received **enlightenment**. Shortly after this he became the Buddha.

A bodhi tree grows today at the spot where Buddhists believe the first one grew.

Buddhists place prayer flags in the tree's branches.

Pilgrims come to the tree to pay respect to the Buddha and to meditate. There are many temples nearby.

A shrine near the bodhi tree at Bodh Gaya

Sarnath

'The place, Ananda, at which "... the wheel of the **Dharma** was set in motion by the Buddha" is a spot to be visited with feelings of reverence.'

The Buddha preached his first sermon in the Deer Park at **Sarnath**. He explained his teachings about the causes and the cure of suffering. The holy men, who at first had left him, became his first disciples (see page 10).

Kusingara

'The place, Ananda, at which "... the Buddha passed finally away" is a spot to be visited with feelings of reverence.'

The Buddha ate the meal that caused his death at the house of **Chunda** (see page 10–11). For Buddhists this is a very holy place. This is because the Buddha completed his personal journey to **nirvana** here.

Learning about religion

❶ Give three reasons why **pilgrimage** is important to Buddhists.

❷ Which is the most important of the four places named in this unit? Why is this?

❸ 'You cannot really understand **Buddhism** until you've been to the places where it started.' What do you think? What might a Buddhist say?

Learning from religion

❶ 'All life is a pilgrimage.' What do you think this means? How far do you think it is true?

❷ Write about a place that is very special for you. Give reasons why it is so special.

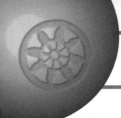

Living in a monastery

In this section you will:

● learn about the importance of monastic life in Buddhism

● think about self-discipline.

Joining a monastery

There are Buddhist monasteries in many countries. There are some in Great Britain.

In some Buddhist countries, such as Thailand, boys may become a **monk** for a short time. This enables them to get a good education, because **monasteries** are places to learn. They also gain good **karma** for themselves and their families.

They can stay in the **monastery** and go to a special school for advanced education. If a boy wants to become a fully adult member of the community, he goes through two stages:

➊ **Samanera** – this is the name given to a **novice**. He is 'on probation' to see if he is suited to the life of a monk.

A boy's head is shaved as he joins a monastery

➋ **Bhikkhu** – after the age of 20 a young man can make a promise to stay a monk for the rest of his life. A bhikkhu is an adult who is training for the monastic life.

A person has to pass many tests before he can be fully accepted into the life of a monk.

What effect does joining a monastery have?

Once a man decides to be **ordained** as a monk, he must have his head and all facial hair shaved. This is a sign that the monk has put aside vanity.

He then receives a robe from the community. The community also gives him an **alms** bowl, or 'begging bowl'. In Thailand the community gives him sandals, needle and thread, a string of beads, a razor and an umbrella. He also receives a net to drain out insects from his drinking water. British monks own their own robe and bowl.

At the ceremony of **ordination**, five monks show the boundaries of the monastery. The candidate kneels in front of the senior monk, usually called the abbot.

He asks the abbot if he can become a monk. The abbot recites a **meditation** about human life and the fact that it is perishable. The candidate asks for forgiveness. He promises to be humble, to be committed to the **Buddha**, **Dharma** and the **Sangha**, and to follow the rules of the monastery.

He has to state that his parents know he wants to be a monk and accept his choice. He has to state that he is a free man

The things a monk can own

Life in a monastery

Monks may live in small huts in the forest, or help to run the local **vihara**. In large monasteries, they may help to run the school.

In Britain, both men and women can be ordained. Women are called **nuns**.

Nuns have to follow many of the same rules as the monks, including shaving their heads. They may share a monastery with monks, or live in a separate building.

without debt and employment. He has to show that he is human and a male.

The abbot gives him a Buddhist name. It is usually one that relates to a personal quality that the candidate could develop.

Chithurst Monastery in Sussex

Learning about religion

❶ Why do you think people choose to become monks?

❷ Use information from this page and page 42–3 to write a radio item to try to encourage people to become Buddhist monks and nuns.

Learning from religion

❶ If you could only own ten things, what would they be, and why?

❷ 'Being a monk is running away, not trying to help the world.' How might a Buddhist monk answer this? What do you think?

❸ Write two lists labelled 'plus' and 'minus'. Put in each the *pluses* and *minuses* of living life as a monk.

Being in a community

In this section you will:
- learn more about living in a monastery
- learn why this is important to Buddhists today.

Following the rules

Most games and sports have rules. It would be impossible to play without them.

Drivers who ignore 'the rules of the road' cause accidents, and people are hurt.

We may not *like* rules but we *need* them to enjoy the best of life.

The intentions of a monastery

Buddhists have to follow the **Five Moral Precepts** (see page 14). **Monks** and **nuns** have extra precepts called 'Intentions'. These include:

1. not to over-eat
2. not to sing, dance or attend entertainments
3. not to wear jewellery, perfume or beauty products
4. not to sleep in a high or wide bed
5. not to handle money.

Some of the things a monk has to give up

These **Vinaya**, or intentions, are part of the training system. They are not rules to keep monks and nuns under control. Rather, they are part of the training to be free from desire. Their lifestyle has to be simple, without luxury. They have only the basics of food, shelter and medicine.

If monks or nuns wear jewellery, perfume or flowers, they are attracting attention to themselves.

The **alms** bowl is where Buddhists place gifts of food for the monks. Monks are not allowed to receive money directly. Other Buddhists can give all kinds of practical help for the work of the **monastery**.

Each monastery and convent may have its own **precepts**. These may overlap with the precepts of other communities. The Theravadin Vinaya follow 227 precepts, but the Zen or Tibetan Vinaya may have differences.

These include five important precepts. These are:

1 Kindness – not to hurt a living thing.

2 Honesty – not to take what is not given.

3 **Celibacy** – not to take part in any sexual act.

4 Truthfulness – not to give offence in speech.

5 Clear-mindedness – not to take drugs or alcohol that could cloud the mind.

Daily life in the monastery

At the Chithurst Monastery, the day begins at 5.00am. The monks chant (recite sections of the scriptures) and meditate. They have breakfast and carry out some morning duties before the next **meditation** at 7.30am.

During the morning there is a meeting to decide who will carry out various jobs. They have the main meal of the day at 10.30am. They have a short rest, then carry out more tasks. In the afternoon they have a cup of tea. They do not have any more food after the 10.30am main meal. Usually, the community goes to bed at 9.00pm, but sometimes chanting and meditation lasts through the night.

Learning about religion

1 Why do you think monasteries have the precepts they have?

2 Make a list of rules that you think would be more relevant today. Discuss these in class.

3 How do you think monks help the Buddhist community? Try using the Internet to connect you to Buddhist websites.

Learning from religion

1 'Spending all day meditating is a waste of time.' What might a Buddhist monk say to this? What do you think? Give reasons for your answer.

2 'Living with other people helps you to become a better person.' How true do you think this is?

3 'Rules are not really necessary when people try not to be selfish.' What do you think of this?

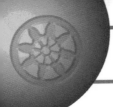

Birth

In this section you will:

- find out how some Buddhists celebrate the birth of children
- think about the importance of the birth of a new baby.

Birthdays

Most people enjoy birthday celebrations. They love to receive presents and cards and to know that other people care about them.

Birth ceremonies in Buddhism

Many Buddhists hold a birth blessing to mark the birth of a child. They bless the child when he or she comes into the world. The naming ceremony comes later.

In Mynamar the family joins together to celebrate the birth of the baby. They give the baby a cradle, and put gifts in it.

The family chooses useful presents. For a little boy there may be books, hammers and tools. A girl may receive sewing thread and needles.

Birthdays can be important celebrations

Importance of family life for the Buddha

The **Buddha** believed that people need family life to enable them to grow as individuals.

He compared the family to a group of trees in the forest. They support each other and give protection against the wind. He said we need our families to help us.

A child is very precious to its parents

In some Buddhist countries, they may shave the baby's hair off when he or she is a month old. They believe shaving the hair is a symbol of a new start. Other Buddhists think that this is just superstition.

Families invite **monks** to the birthday party. They may choose a name for the child which is a symbol of the qualities that the family would like the child to develop. They may name the child after a famous Buddhist from the past. The monks will usually chant scriptures for the child.

In some Buddhist countries, a sacred thread is wound around the wrist of the child. This is a sign of blessing.

The **Theravada** monks may sprinkle the child with water. This again is a sign of a blessing for the future. They may drip wax from a pure white candle into the water. This is a sign of the four natural elements of earth, air, fire and water.

Learning about religion

❶ Why do you think birth ceremonies are important to Buddhists? Give reasons.

❷ 'Buddhist birth ceremonies are sexist.' How might a Buddhist answer this?

❸ Design a leaflet for a Buddhist temple to give out to explain about Buddhist birth ceremonies. Use information from a Buddhist Internet site or CD-ROM.

Learning from religion

❶ Do you think everyone – both religious and non-religious – should have a naming ceremony? Explain your answer.

❷ Working in a group, write your own birth ceremony. Act it out in class.

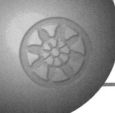

Marriage

In this section you will:

- learn about the importance of marriage to Buddhists
- think about the importance of commitment.

Committed for life?

For many people, marriage is a way of saying publicly that you intend to stay together in a loving relationship. People make promises before their family, friends and the community. People who believe in God make these promises before God. Unfortunately, not all marriages last.

Many people decide to live with a partner without being married. They say that it is not necessary to visit a holy building or a registry office. They can be just as committed without the ceremony.

Marriage in Buddhist countries

Buddhist countries differ in their marriage customs. Some things remain the same. In some Buddhist countries marriages are 'arranged'. This means that the parents of the couple get together to set up the marriage. In other Buddhist countries the couple arrange their own marriage.

In Thailand, the wedding takes place in the bride's home. The family invites **monks** to come to bless the couple and recite scriptures for them. Monks do not

A Buddhist wedding

A monk can bless the newly married couple

actually perform the ceremony. A relative, such as the uncle or grandfather of the bride does this.

British Buddhists may be married in a registry office, and then blessed afterwards. The couple stands on a special platform called a **purowa**. It is decorated with white flowers.

During the ceremony, the couple exchange rings and make **vows** to each other. The person performing the ceremony wraps a silk scarf around their hands. This is a way of saying that they have now been joined together as husband and wife.

In a **Theravada** wedding, they pass a thread of cotton around the temple where the wedding is taking place. The husband cuts the thread and a monk wraps it around the wrist of the bridegroom. The bridegroom then places the other piece of thread round the wrist of his bride.

As in most countries, it is a tradition that after the wedding ceremony there is a big feast. The family pays for this and invite all friends and family members.

Learning about religion

❶ Use the Internet to find out more about Buddhist weddings. Use this information to write a short talk about Buddhist weddings.

❷ Explain some of the symbols in a Buddhist marriage.

❸ 'The **Buddha** did not show any commitment to his own marriage. He left his wife when he took up a holy life.' What would a Buddhist say about this? What would you say?

Learning from religion

❶ Write in two columns what you think may be the advantages and disadvantages of arranged marriages.

❷ 'Marriage is old-fashioned and out-of-date.' Arrange a class discussion about this.

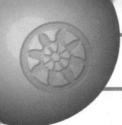

Death

In this section you will:
● learn about Buddhist beliefs concerning death and learn about Buddhist funeral rites
● think about dealing with death and bereavement.

Buddhist funerals

Buddhist funerals are different in different countries.

In Sri Lanka, the family arranging the funeral must first wash the body. Then they arrange the hands so that they are clasped together. They wind a thread

A Buddhist cemetery

A Buddhist funeral procession in Myanmar (Burma)

three times round the hands. This is a sign of the three things that 'tied' the dead person to this world: money, marriage and children.

They place other things in the coffin:

1. a small ladder as a sign that the mind will leave the body

2. flowers and incense as signs that life does not last and must end in death

3. a small set of flags to help the person's arrival in the heavens.

Funerals usually take place in the local **monastery**. Buddhists are **cremated** on a funeral **pyre**.

Later a **monk** gathers the ashes of the dead person and recites verses from scripture about how short life is.

The monk may arrange some of the bone fragments in a half circle, running from west to east. This shows the reality of life and death. Then he collects up the pieces of bone and ash in an **urn** and buries it.

A relic of a specially holy or famous person may be placed in a **stupa**.

Funerals in Mahayana countries

Buddhists in China, Taiwan and Korea honour their dead ancestors. The monk places a tablet, which is a small piece of ivory, wood or polished stone, in their memory on the family shrine in their home.

The monk washes the body before the funeral ceremony.

Friends and neighbours often celebrate with a meal. They burn incense in the graveyard.

Families keep up a long period of **mourning** for their dead relatives. They believe this will gain **merit** for the person who has died.

Relatives may make gifts to the monks for their help and support during this time.

A Buddhist poet wrote:

No weeping, nor yet sorrowing,
Nor any kind of mourning aids,
Departed one, whose kin remain,
(Unhelped by their action) thus.

(from *Minor Readings* by Bhikku Naranoni)

Learning about religion

1. Write about the important symbols in a Buddhist funeral in Sri Lanka.

2. How do monks help Buddhists with the funerals of their loved ones?

3. Why do you think washing the body is so important to Buddhists?

Learning from religion

1. Should a funeral help you to celebrate a life, or to mourn the death of a loved one? Give reasons for your answer.

2. Write a poem about the life of someone you know who has died.

The environment

In this section you will:

● learn about Buddhist ideas about the environment

● think about important issues concerning the environment.

What a wonderful world

We live in a beautiful world. However, human beings have damaged the world. We have used aerosols that help to cause the Greenhouse Effect. This is causing climate change.

Oil tankers have leaked and ruined parts of the sea and coastlines. Many birds and other wildlife have died as a result.

Human beings make decisions which can spoil the world we live in.

Do no harm

Buddhists believe that they should do no harm to any living thing. This is called **ahimsa**.

Many Buddhists do all they can to avoid killing any form of life. They may use a strainer to avoid accidentally swallowing insects. Or they may lay a trail of sugar to

Pollution can damage the earth

lead ants out of the kitchen. This means they do not have to put down ant powder to kill them.

So who made the earth?

Buddhists say that it is impossible to know if there is a creator God who made the planet. This is because they do not have first-hand experience of this.

However, they believe that it is a human duty to create a better world through wise choices and harmless living.

Karma

As we have seen, Buddhists believe that all actions cause effects. This means that if people live in a way that damages others, this causes effects for themselves and the planet.

Groups of humans can also affect the **environment**. People need to encourage their governments and other groups to act responsibly.

Do not take what is not given

One of the **Five Moral Precepts** (see page 14–15) that the **Buddha** gave to his followers said that they should not take what is not given to them.

This affects the Buddhist thinking about the environment. They do not abuse the environment. If they have to take something they will put it back. For example, if they cut down a tree, a Buddhist would plant another tree to replace it.

Buddhists teach that all of nature is interconnected. People need to take care of it, because human beings are also an important part of nature.

Learning about religion

❶ What does ahimsa mean? How does this affect the way Buddhists treat the environment?

❷ Use the Internet to try to find out more about Buddhist beliefs and the environment. Use this to write a leaflet for a Buddhist environmental group.

Learning from religion

❶ 'Do not take what is not given.' In terms of the environment, how might this teaching be put into practice by: **a** individuals, **b** companies, **c** countries?

❷ 'Buddhists are so interested in **nirvana**, they don't really care about the world.' How would a Buddhist react to this? What do you think? Show that you have considered more than one point of view.

❸ Draw a diagram to show how one person's actions can affect the environment.

Wealth and poverty

In this section you will:
● learn about the Buddhist attitudes to wealth and poverty
● think about these issues as they affect the world today.

One world?

Economists (people who study how money is made and spent) say that the world can be divided into two main groups.

1 Developed nations – these are the countries that depend on industry and are very rich, for example Britain, the USA, Germany, and Australia.

2 Developing nations – these are sometimes very poor.

In Developing nations, 19,000 children die every day from hunger. Millions of children die before their fifth birthdays, often of diseases such as measles.

Buddhist teaching on wealth and poverty

Siddhartha's family was very rich, but he chose to live in the same way as the poor holy men he met on his visits to the city. (see pages 6–7).

He realised that being rich or poor, or enjoying pleasure or enduring pain, would not lead him to the truth.

The **Buddha** taught that people should follow a **Middle Way** between these extremes. Buddhists today would say that

Buddhism teaches care of the poor

The Buddha shows compassion

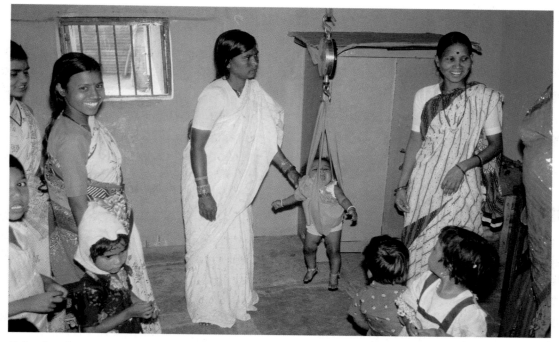

Bringing hope and healing

we need a balance: enough food for everyone's *need*, but not enough for their *greed*.

The Buddha also taught that 'Desire leads to pain.' The rich nations need to think about the victims of their greed. That is, they should think about the poor people who have to work for next to nothing so that the rich can buy cheap foreign produce.

Engaged Buddhism

The Buddhist **monk** Tich Nhat Hanh from Vietnam taught that **Buddhism** is a way of 'engaging with life'. The aim of Buddhism is to find inner peace. This involves thinking about the consequences of their actions. They believe that if they are aware of their intentions (for example to help or not to help a person) **karma** will result.

Many British Buddhists support the **Karuna** Trust. This organization helps to care for and feed the poorest people in those countries.

Learning about religion

❶ How does the Middle Way affect the way Buddhists think about wealth and poverty?

❷ Using the Internet, find out more about the work of the Karuna Trust. Write a leaflet to advertise its work.

Learning from religion

❶ 'Selfishness is the real reason why people are poor.' How true is this saying? Explain your answer. What else do you think leads to people being poor?

❷ What do you think you could do to help the poor in the world?

Racism

In this section you will:

● learn about the Buddhist teaching on racism and prejudice

● reflect on attitudes to racism.

All the same?

We are all different. Many people have **prejudices** about others. That is, they pre-judge individuals and groups. They make up their minds about someone before they even meet them.

They may form **stereotypes** of people. A stereotype is a kind of mental picture which says that a whole group of people behaves in the same way. For example, 'All children are a nuisance,' or 'all old people are bad-tempered.'

Some people are prejudiced against those of a different race. They apply stereotypes to racial groups. Prejudice and stereotyping can lead to **discrimination**. Discrimination on grounds of race is racism. It is unfair treatment.

If a person in a position of power stops a person getting something they are entitled to because of prejudice, this is discrimination. For example, an employer might refuse to employ a woman or a person from a racial minority group. The law says this is wrong, but it still happens.

Stereotyping: forming a mental picture of what people should be like

Buddhism teaches compassion and love

How a Buddhist sees racism

Buddhism says that racism is '**unskilful**'.

The **Buddha** taught that there are poisons that can cloud the mind. Ignorance and arrogance are two of these poisons.

In the **Eightfold Path** (see page 9), he taught the need to follow the way of Right Understanding. To judge someone by the colour of their skin, or where their parents were born, shows ignorance and leads to suffering.

In the **Four Noble Truths** (see page 9), the Buddha taught that people should get away from ideas about self. To be racist is to say that one 'self' is better than another.

Buddhism encourages its followers to develop loving kindness to all living things. This is called **metta**.

Learning about religion

❶ Which Buddhist teachings do you think might be most helpful to overcome racism?

❷ 'No Buddhist should ever be racist.' Write an advert for a TV or Radio station in a Buddhist country to show how racism is wrong.

Learning from religion

❶ What do you think makes people racist? List as many ideas as you can.

❷ Does religion stop or encourage racism? Give reasons.

Key figures 1

In this section you will:

- learn about the life and teaching of the Dalai Lama
- understand why he is so important to Buddhists today.

A special boy

Buddhists in Tibet have always had a leader with the title **Dalai Lama**. They believe that the Dalai Lama is the **reincarnation** of a **Bodhisattva** (see page 24). That is, an enlightened being who chooses to be re-born to help others to find the truth.

In 1940, a young boy called Tenzin Gyasto was chosen as the new Dalai Lama. He became both the religious leader and head of the country of Tibet. When he became the Dalai Lama he was so young that other people had to help him to rule.

The Chinese invasion

In 1950, the Chinese army invaded Tibet. The Chinese government wanted Tibet to become a province of China. They took control of the country. In the capital city, Lhasa, many Tibetans rebelled against the Chinese. The Chinese executed thousands of these rebels.

The Dalai Lama fled across the border to India. He thought that he could help the Tibetans best by remaining free. He knew the Chinese would either arrest him or kill him if he remained in Tibet.

The Chinese attacked the monasteries in Tibet and destroyed their holy books. They would not listen to the Tibetans. They believed that they were setting the Tibetans free from pointless, evil laws.

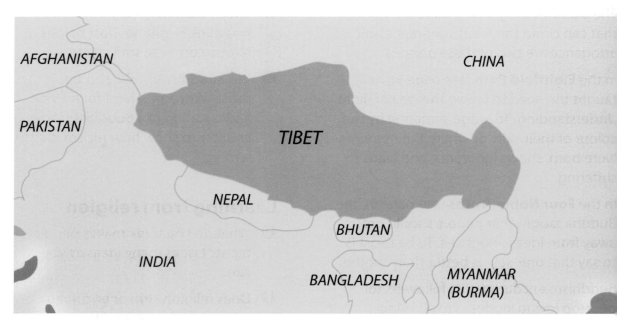

Tibet today

He has written:

'Today we depend on each other and we are closely connected with each other. This means we are responsible for one another. We must have a feeling of being brothers and sisters. We are all members of one human family. If we do not believe this, we cannot hope to mend the damage to our existence – let alone bring peace and happiness'.

One person who has been influenced by the Dalai Lama is the film actor Richard Gere. He established the Gere Foundation and has organized public events to highlight Tibet's problems.

The Dalai Lama

When Chairman Mao, the Chinese ruler, died in 1976, Lhasa was in ruins.

A man of peace

The Dalai Lama is a man of peace. Despite the invasion of his country, he refuses to advise a violent response to what has happened.

He has listened to what the Chinese had to say. He says that the political beliefs of China and of Tibetan **Buddhism** do not have to be at war.

He has travelled the world, speaking on behalf of the Tibetan people. He calls for peace in the world. He has been to Britain and made broadcasts on TV and radio.

Learning about religion

❶ Why is the Dalai Lama so special to Tibetan Buddhists? Give as many reasons as you can.

❷ Using books from the school library, or a visit to the Internet, design a wall-display to show the history and traditions of Tibet.

Learning from religion

❶ Should the Tibetans have used violence against the Chinese to get their freedom back? Give reasons for your answer.

❷ Find out more about the Nobel Prize and people who have received this award. Write about what you have found out.

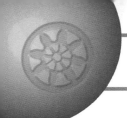

Key figures 2

A monk's tale

Ajahn Sumedho is the leader of a group of Buddhist **monks**. They are **Theravadan** monks, and have monasteries in the UK, Italy, Switzerland, Thailand, North America, Australia and New Zealand.

Ajahn Sumedho was born in Seattle in the USA in 1934. His original name was Robert Jackson. He was brought up a Christian, but became interested in the ideas and religions of the Far East. In 1963, he obtained a qualification in Far Eastern Studies and went to work as a teacher in Borneo.

He visited Thailand in 1966, and decided to become a monk. In 1976, he became leader of the British Buddhist community.

Sumedho wrote his autobiography (life story). In it he said how important **Buddhism** was to him, and how it helped him to understand how the world works.

'The mind is like a mirror; it has the ability to reflect things. Mirrors reflect anything – beautiful or ugly, good or bad. And those things do not harm the mirror.'

In other words, we cannot be harmed by our minds. He also wrote:

We observe. "This is how our lives have to be." Then we wisely use what we have, learn from it and free ourself from the narrow limits of self and mortality.

Ajahn Sumedho

A politician's story

In the elections of 1989, 80 per cent of the voters chose **Aung San Suu Kyi** as the leader of Myanmar (Burma).

The army did not like this result, and placed her under house arrest. They said the elections did not count and they were still in power.

The reason the army did not like her was that she had said the army was corrupt (bad) and treated the Burmese people unfairly.

Aung San Suu Kyi

Her political party, the National League for Democracy, was banned. The army did not let her leave the country, even when her husband was dying of cancer. He was in Britain, where she had lived for several years. He died in 1999.

As a Buddhist, Aung San Suu Kyi told her people that they must try to persuade the army to accept the results of the election by non-violent means. She pointed to the example of the Indian Hindu leader, Mahatma Gandhi, and the Christian civil rights leader, Martin Luther King.

She organized sit-ins and peaceful protests in order to bring about peace and democracy.

Learning about religion

❶ What do you think might have attracted someone like Ajahn Sumedho to Buddhism?

❷ See what you can find about Aung San Suu Kyi on the Internet. Working with others, plan a wall display about her life and beliefs.

Learning from religion

❶ Look up what you can find about Martin Luther King in the USA and Mahatma Gandhi in India. With this information, organise a class discussion on the following topic: 'Can non-violence work against a tyrannical and unfair government?'

❷ Find out about the work of Amnesty International on the Internet. Visit their Website. Then write a leaflet to introduce their work to someone of your age.

Glossary

Abhidharma Pitaka Teachings from the Three Baskets about the way the world is

Ahimsa 'Harmlessness', doing no harm to any living creature

Agnostic Someone who thinks it is not possible to know whether a god exists

Alms Gifts of charity

Ananda The Buddha's successor in leading the Buddhist community

Archaeologists People who study items from past times to find out about the history of that time

Asceticism Belief that by punishing the body one can get to spiritual truth

Avalokitesvara A Bodhisattva who represents perfect compassion

Bhikkhu A monk who makes a life-long commitment

Bodh Gaya Place where Buddha became enlightened

Bodhisattvas 'Buddha's to be.' Spiritual beings who choose to help people though they could go on to nirvana

Brahma Viharas Qualities to be developed through meditation

Buddha The Enlightened or Awakened one. Title given to Siddhartha Gautama after his enlightenment

Buddhism The religion taught by the Buddha

Celibacy Avoiding sexual acts

Channa The chariot driver who took Siddhartha to the city and to the forest

Chunda Owner of the house where the Buddha ate food that poisoned him

Compassionate Caring, kind-hearted

Cremation The custom of burning the bodies of dead people to ash

Dalai Lama Spiritual leader of Tibetan Buddhists

Dana Generosity

Devotion Loyalty, showing respect

Dharmapada A collection of the Buddha's sayings, a Buddhist scripture

Dharma 'Universal Truth', one of the teachings of the Buddha

Dhyana Concentration

Discrimination Treating people unfairly because of prejudice (racial, sexual or other)

Eightfold Path Steps that will lead to freedom from the idea of 'self' and will help the Buddhist to reach nirvana

Engaged Buddhism The idea that Buddhism should engage (get involved with) the political and social questions of the world

Enlightenment Understanding of what is true and what is not. To find the path to truth

Environment Natural surroundings

Five Moral Precepts Five moral intentions that Buddhists try to follow in their lives

Four Noble Truths The teaching of the Buddha on suffering, its causes and its solutions

Jataka Tales Collection of stories about the Buddha's previous lives

Karma Buddhist belief that all actions have consequences

Karuna Compassionate love for others

Kisagami A female follower of the Buddha. Many believe she formed an order of Buddhist nuns

Kshanti Patience

Kusingara Where the Buddha died

Lotus flower Symbol of enlightenment

Lotus Sutra A key teaching of the Buddha

Lumbini Grove Where the Buddha was born, according to legend

Mahayana Buddhism One of two branches of Buddhism. They stress the importance of Bodhisattvas

Maitreya A Bodhisattva who will bring a golden age in the future

Mala Beads A string of 108 beads that some Buddhists use to help them to meditate

Mandalas Images, often made of sand, to help Buddhists to understand the changing nature of life

Mantra A short sentence saying something important about religion

Mara A devil-like figure who tried to stop Siddhartha from becoming the Buddha

Mayadevi Queen of the Saykas, and the Buddha's mother

Meditation Thinking deeply for religious reasons. Mental practice to help to reach enlightenment

Merit A deed that adds to good karma

Metta Loving kindness

Middle Way The Buddha's teaching that life must be a balance between pleasure and pain in order to find the way to enlightenment

Monastery A place where monks live

Monk A man who gives up ordinary life to live a completely religious life

Mourn To express sorrow at the death of a loved one

Mudita Sympathetic joy

Nagasena Buddhist thinker who compared the self to a chariot

Nirvana 'Emptiness'. The goal of Buddhism to become one with the universe and no longer bound up with suffering and existence

Novice A 'trainee' monk or nun

Nun A woman who gives up her ordinary life to live a religious life

Obon Japanese festival, connected with devotion to ancestors

Ordained/ordination A formal ceremony to accept a person into a religious life

Pagoda (Dagoda) Buddhist religious building on five levels to show the nature of the universe which has five elements

Pali Canon First, original scripture of Buddhism

Pilgrimage A journey to a special place for religious reasons

Pitaka Collection of scriptures; Vinaya, Sutra, Abhidharma

Prajna Wisdom

Precept A principle or intention for living

Prejudice Pre-judging other people without knowing them

Purowa Platform used for Buddhist weddings

Pyre The stack of wood on which dead bodies are burned

Rahula Son of Siddhartha Gautama. His name means 'Chain'

Refuge Place of safety, protection

Relics Remains of holy people, for example fragments of bone, or pieces of clothing

Reincarnation Re-embodiment, re-birth in human form

Rupas Images used to help Buddhists to meditate and show respect to the Buddha

Samanera Buddhist novice monk

Sangha The Buddhist community, a name sometimes given to a group of monks or nuns

Sarnath The place in the Deer Park where the Buddha gave his first sermon

Saykas The tribe into which the Buddha was born

Siddhartha Gautama 'Perfect Fulfilment'. The name of the person who became known as the Buddha

Sila Morality

Skilful/Unskilful Buddhist ideas about moral action, which are skilful (right) or unskilful (inappropriate or wrong)

Songkran The Thai Buddhist new year festival

Stereotypes Forming mental pictures of the way people behave

Stupa A Buddhist religious building that contains a sacred relic of the Buddha or an important Buddhist

Suddohana King of the Saykas

Sutra Pitaka Collection of speeches and teachings of the Buddha. Part of the scriptures known as the Three Baskets

Tara A Bodhisattva who helps in enlightenment

Theravada One of the two main branches of Buddhism. The word means 'Teaching of the elders'

Three Refuges The three most important things in Buddhism, the Buddha, the Dharma (teaching) and the Sangha (the Buddhist community)

Tripitaka The teaching of the Buddha known as the Three Baskets

Urn A special container for the ashes of a dead person

Vihara Another name for a Buddhist temple

Vinaya Pitaka Part of the Buddhist scriptures that monks and nuns follow

Vow A solemn promise

Wat Name for a Buddhist temple in Thailand

Wesak Festival celebrating the birth, enlightenment and death of the Buddha

Wheel of Life Symbol used to explain how humans are trapped into suffering. Often shown with eight spokes, to show that following the Eightfold Path will help people to escape from this life cycle

Yashodhara Wife of Siddhartha Gautama

Index